CHUCK NORRIS

A Real-Life Reader Biography

Melanie Cole

Mitchell Lane Publishers, Inc.
P.O. Box 200 • Childs, Maryland 21916

Mitchell Lane
PUBLISHERS

Second Printing
Real-Life Reader Biographies

Selena	Robert Rodriguez	Mariah Carey	Rafael Palmeiro
Tommy Nuñez	Trent Dimas	Cristina Saralegui	Andres Galarraga
Oscar De La Hoya	Gloria Estefan	Jimmy Smits	Mary Joe Fernandez
Cesar Chavez	Chuck Norris	Sinbad	Paula Abdul
Vanessa Williams	Celine Dion	Mia Hamm	Michelle Kwan
Brandy	Shania Twain	Garth Brooks	Sammy Sosa
Mark McGwire	Rosie O'Donnell	Jeff Gordon	Salma Hayek
Sheila E.	Hollywood Hogan	Arnold Schwarzenegger	

Library of Congress Cataloging-in-Publication Data
Cole, Melanie. 1957–
    Chuck Norris / Melanie Cole.
      p. cm.—(A real-life reader biography)
    Includes index.
    Summary: A brief biography of the martial arts expert and actor, Chuck Norris.
    ISBN 1-883845-91-2
    1. Norris, Chuck. 1940– —Juvenile literature. 2. Martial artists—United States—Biography—Juvenile literature. 3. Actors—United States—Biography—Juvenile literature. [1. Norris, Chuck, 1940– . 2. Martial artists. 3. Actors and actresses.] I. Title. II. Series.
GV1113.N67C65 1999
796.8'092—dc21
[B]
    98-38129
    CIP
    AC

ABOUT THE AUTHOR: Melanie Cole has been a writer and editor for eighteen years. She was previously an associate editor of *Texas Monthly* and then editor of *Hispanic* magazine. She has published numerous poems, articles, and reviews. She is a contributing writer to the Mitchell Lane series **Famous People of Hispanic Heritage** and has authored several books for children, including **Mary Joe Fernandez** (Mitchell Lane) and **Jimmy Smits** (Mitchell Lane). Originally from Kansas, Ms. Cole now resides in Austin, Texas.

PHOTO CREDITS: cover: Kobal Collection; p. 4 Eric Heinila/Shooting Star; p. 6 Shooting Star; p. 10 Michael Ferguson/Globe Photos; p. 11 courtesy CBS; p. 14 Ralph Dominguez/Globe Photos; p. 18 AP Photo; p. 24, 25 Kobal Collection; p. 27, 29 top & bottom AP Photo; p. 30 M. Neveux/Shooting Star; p. 31 top Archive Photos; bottom, AP Photo.

ACKNOWLEDGMENTS: This story has been thoroughly researched, and to the best of our knowledge, represents a true story. Though we try to authorize every biography that we publish, for various reasons, this is not always possible. This story is neither authorized nor endorsed by Chuck Norris or any of his representatives.

Table of Contents

Chapter 1
A Tough Childhood

Chuck Norris is an action man. He has played a tough guy on television and in the movies. He has spent his entire life studying and practicing the martial arts, earning several black belts and world championships. But beneath the tough man exterior lies a gifted and caring person. The star of the successful TV series, *Walker, Texas Ranger*, Chuck Norris devotes much of his time and energy off the TV set helping kids through his Kick

Chuck Norris has spent his entire life studying the martial arts.

Drugs Out of America campaign, a
nonprofit foundation that he
established in 1990 to help combat
drug use and gang-related violence
in the schools.

*Chuck Norris
teaches kids how
to protect them-
selves and how to
say no to drugs.*

Chuck Norris was born on
March 10, 1940, in the small town of
Ryan, Oklahoma. His parents,
Wilma Scarberry Norris and Ray

Norris, were very young when he was born. He was named Carlos Ray Norris after the family's minister, the Reverend Carlos Berry. His middle name came from his father. Chuck's parents were both half Native American and half Irish American.

In those years before the start of World War II, Chuck's parents were always poor. Before he was 15 years old, the family had moved 13 times. To support his family, Chuck's father worked as a mechanic, a bus driver, and a manual laborer.

Chuck's brother, Wieland, was born in 1942. The two boys were very close as they grew up. When Chuck was six, the family moved to Napa, California, where Wilma worked at an airplane factory and Ray worked in the shipyards. But

Chuck Norris was born in the small town of Ryan, Oklahoma.

Wieland had terrible asthma, so the family moved to Miami, Arizona, to a drier climate. By 1949 the family was back in California again, where they stayed.

Ray Norris was drafted into active military service in World War II. His leg was injured in fighting, and for a time he was missing in action. When he returned home, he had a hard time keeping a job due to his bad leg. He also developed a drinking problem. Because Ray was now unreliable, Wilma had to do whatever she could to earn money.

Chuck learned to help at an early age. In many ways he became the "man" of the family, because his father was seldom around.

In 1951, when Chuck was 11, his mother became pregnant again. By this point, Chuck's father was absent from the family's day-to-day

Ray Norris was drafted into active military service in World War II.

life, visiting only once in a while. Because another baby was on the way, Wilma could not work, so the family of three was forced to go on welfare. Ray's $30-a-month disability check was just enough to cover the rent.

Even though times were hard, Wilma looked on the bright side. Chuck remembered, "Mom accepted things as they were and was determined to make the best of the situation. Her love and devotion for Wieland and me made our lack of material possessions seem insignificant." Chuck, too, learned to make the most of a bad situation, which would help him deal with problems he encountered later as an adult.

The third Norris boy, Aaron, was born in November 1951 in California. Chuck helped his

"Mom accepted things the way they were and was determined to make the best of the situation," says Chuck.

Chuck with brother, Aaron.

mother with the new baby, often caring for him while Wilma worked at the airplane factory. The next year, when Chuck was 12, the family settled in Torrance, California, a city south of Los Angeles. There Chuck and Weiland went to high school.

Wilma and Ray were divorced in 1956. Chuck's mother married a man named George Wright, who was a loving stepfather to the boys.

During his junior year at North Torrance High School, Chuck started dating Dianne Holechek, an outgoing, pretty blond girl. He joined the air force after he graduated from high school in 1958. He and Dianne were married in December of that year.

Chapter 2
Karate Expert

Almost everyone knows Chuck Norris as the star of *Walker, Texas Ranger.* But long before the *Walker* television series, Chuck was a famous karate expert. Fighters in karate use only their hands and feet for self-defense. In Japanese, the word *karate* means "the art of empty hands," for karate artists do not use any weapons.

When he was assigned to Osan Air Force Base in Korea, Chuck wanted to be a military

Chuck Norris stars as the hero in Walker, Texas Ranger.

policeman. But he was a skinny, five-foot-ten kid. He decided that to be respected as a policeman, he needed to get serious about self-defense. He started looking into the martial arts.

His first lessons were in judo, but after breaking his shoulder, he switched to karate. Training to become a karate master was hard, but he didn't give up. Chuck remembers, "Despite the agony of training, I said to myself, 'If I can stick with this, I can stick with anything.'"

Chuck earned his black belt. In karate, belt colors are like school levels. The white belt is similar to beginner level. Other colors represent higher levels of expertise. In Korea, Chuck started using what would become a trademark move: the spinning back kick. This kick was a highlight in his many tournament bouts. It would also be seen by millions of his fans in his movies.

Chuck was honorably discharged from the air force in 1962 and returned to the United States. In the 1960s, when martial arts were just becoming popular in America, he was already an experienced fighter. He studied Tang Soo Do, Tae Kwan Do, karate, and became familiar with all forms of the martial arts. His first major tournament win was the 1965 Winter Nationals in San Jose, California. After that he won many other titles, including the International Grand Championships in Long Beach and the All-American New York Grand Championships. He won the National Tournament of

He studied Tang Soo Do, Tae Kwan Do, and karate.

Champions in Washington, D.C.,
and became *Black Belt* magazine's
Fighter of the Year for 1969. He won
the Professional World
Middleweight title in 1968 at New
York's Madison Square Garden.

With son, Mike

Besides being a fighter, he also
became a teacher of karate, he ran

several martial arts schools where he taught, and he became one of the sport's main organizers. Chuck cofounded the Four Seasons Karate Championships, one of the most successful tournament formats in the sport's history. He also served in the mid-1970s as the commissioner of the newly formed National Karate League.

Chuck and Dianne eventually had two sons. The oldest, Mike, was born in 1963, and the other, Eric, was born in 1965. Both boys were trained by their father in karate, and both have won titles in the martial arts.

Besides being a fighter, Chuck also became a teacher of karate.

Chapter 3
Master
Teacher

Chuck Norris taught karate to many of the TV stars of the 1970s.

One day in 1972, Chuck was about to start a karate class at his school when he received a phone call. The caller, Steve McQueen, said he'd like to bring his son to Chuck's school for lessons. McQueen was a well-known movie star of such films as *Bullitt, The Getaway,* and *The Great Escape.* After his son had taken a few lessons, McQueen decided he wanted to take lessons himself. He and Chuck became good friends.

Chuck also taught karate to many TV stars of the '70s, and some of them also became his friends. His students included Priscilla Presley (Elvis Presley's wife, who starred on TV's *Dallas*), the Osmond family, and Bob Barker (the host of the television game show *Truth or Consequences*). One of the stars of the western series *Bonanza*, Dan Blocker, who played Dan Cartwright, saw Norris in a karate tournament and asked him to teach his children. Through Blocker, Norris met Michael Landon, who played Little Joe Cartwright on *Bonanza*.

Chuck invented his own style of karate, called *chun kuk do*. With this style—using both hands and both feet equally—he won the world title. During the whole time he competed, he was never

Some of his students included Priscilla Presley, the Osmond family, and Bob Barker.

defeated in a bout. He was world middleweight champion in karate for six years running, from 1968 through 1974.

In the mid-1970s, Chuck Norris prepared for a new career in acting.

By the time he retired from the sport in 1974, he had established 32 karate schools. But the schools

developed problems. They were mismanaged by a group of investors who were supposed to be keeping good financial records and paying taxes. Chuck took back control of his schools, but he didn't realize they were in so much trouble. Even so, Chuck refused to declare bankruptcy, something people sometimes do to wipe out their debts. Instead, he closed the schools and sold almost everything he owned to pay off the schools' debts.

These hard times taught Chuck a big lesson. "You know, it's funny how things happen," he told a writer for the *Chicago Tribune.* "If I hadn't lost my schools, I wouldn't have tried acting. I thought the worst thing in the world had happened to me, but it was really a blessing in disguise. . . . One door closes, and a bigger one opens. I really believe that."

"One door closes, and a bigger one opens. I really believe that."

Chapter 4
Man of the Movies

"You ought to pursue an acting career," Steve McQueen told Chuck.

"You ought to pursue an acting career. I think you'd be good at it," Steve McQueen told Chuck. With McQueen's encouragement, Chuck decided to take the plunge into acting. He followed McQueen's advice to go with action movies. Chuck's first movie role came in the Dean Martin film *The Wrecking Crew* in 1969. He spoke one line in the movie, in which he played a bodyguard.

Another friend who encouraged Chuck was the karate

filmmaker Bruce Lee. After *The Wrecking Crew,* Chuck played Bruce Lee's enemy in *Return of the Dragon,* which was filmed mostly in Hong Kong but included a fight scene shot in the Colosseum in Rome. Chuck's defeat by Bruce Lee in the now-famous scene was the first and the last time he was ever beaten on film. Chuck also had a small part in *Game of Death,* the movie Lee was making at the time of his death in 1973. Because of his roles in martial arts movies, Chuck was known for a time as the "blond Bruce Lee." After these action roles, Chuck was cast in 1977's *Breaker! Breaker!* For his next movie, Chuck wanted to make a film that would show a positive role model for young people. He wanted to portray a strong man of few words, similar to the Western heroes he had seen in

Chuck played Bruce Lee's enemy in *Return of the Dragon.*

movies as a child. He found that role in *Good Guys Wear Black.*

Released in 1979, the movie was the first film in which Norris played a Vietnam veteran. Chuck played these kinds of roles because they were close to his heart. His brother Wieland had been killed in Vietnam in 1970.

In *A Force of One*, released in 1979, Chuck played a Vietnam Special Forces veteran who teaches martial arts to a squad in California. *The Octagon,* which came out in 1980, was about a Central American terrorist group. With these three U.S. martial arts films—*Good Guys Wear Black, A Force of One,* and *The Octagon*—Chuck started making much more money, and the movies each earned more than $100 million. Next came *An Eye for an Eye* in 1981. In this film, Chuck played a former

His brother Wieland was killed in Vietnam in 1970.

San Francisco undercover cop. In *Silent Rage* (1982), which he starred in and coproduced, he got rid of a crazed killer and a gang of cruel bikers. In *Forced Vengeance* (1982), he played the security chief of a Hong Kong casino. The first movie in which Chuck didn't rely heavily on karate was *Lone Wolf McQuade*, released in 1983. The movie did very well at the box office.

Other big hits followed, notably *Invasion U.S.A.* (1985) and *The Delta Force* (1986). In 1986 he also appeared in *Firewalker*, and in 1988, *Hero and the Terror*. Chuck also finished his three-movie tribute to his brother Wieland. In these films—*Missing in Action, Missing in Action 2: The Beginning*, and *Braddock: Missing in Action III*—Chuck played Colonel James Braddock, who returns to Vietnam

Chuck took on several Vietnam movies as a tribute to his brother.

to rescue American prisoners of war.

Chuck's more recent movies have shown him in a wider variety of roles. He released *Delta Force 2* in 1990, *The Hitman* in 1991, *Sidekicks* in 1993, *Hellbound* in 1994, and *Top Dog* in 1995. *Sidekicks* is about a young boy who, with Chuck

Chuck Norris played Colonel Scott McCoy in Delta Force 2.

Norris's help, uses martial arts to stand up to a bully. In the funny family movie *Top Dog*, Chuck's police companion is a dog named Reno.

Chuck Norris with his police dog companion, Reno, from the movie, Top Dog.

Chapter 5
Walker
Reaches Out

From *Lone Wolf McQuade*, Chuck Norris became *Walker, Texas Ranger*.

It wasn't much of a stretch from *Lone Wolf McQuade* to *Walker, Texas Ranger*. McQuade was a bearded Texas ranger who fought against an evil arms dealer. In the CBS television series *Walker, Texas Ranger,* Norris plays Cordell Walker, a member of a group of law enforcement officers based in Dallas. The series surprised everyone when it placed in the top ten shows in 1993, its first year. Every Saturday night the five-foot-ten, 170-pound actor with sandy hair and a reddish brown beard plays the modern-day Western hero Walker. The show tackles many of the problems of our times. In every episode, Walker defends people who have had something bad happen to them. Kids like the show because Walker is a good man. They can look up to him and his fellow rangers. Though critics have said his show is too violent, Chuck insists that the action

Chuck Norris uses a karate move as he wields a knife to cut a cake celebrating the 100th episode of "Walker, Texas Ranger." (L to R): Clarence Gilyard, Chuck Norris, Noble Willingham, and Chuck's brother, producer Aaron Norris.

sequences are an integral part of the show. "It's not fighting for fighting's sake," he says. "There is morality behind the violence."

From 1993 through 1998, Walker was one of the most-watched family shows on television.

Chuck stays close to his family, even in his work. His youngest brother, Aaron, started working on the show in late 1995. Aaron directed seven of Chuck's movies, and the two work well together. Chuck and Dianne were divorced in 1989, but he stayed close to his children. Eric, Chuck's youngest son, directs the action segments that require stunts. Chuck's older son, Mike, an actor and producer who lives in Chicago, also sometimes appears on *Walker*.

Just as Chuck hopes to always portray heroes in his film and television roles, he wants to be heroic in his day-to-day life. In August 1990, Chuck formed the Kick Drugs Out of America

Aaron Norris, Chuck's brother, directs many of his movies and the show, *Walker, Texas Ranger*.

Foundation, a project that is very important to him. The idea behind the foundation is to teach kids karate. Through karate, the kids get the self-esteem and discipline necessary to say no to drugs and stay out of gangs.

It is important for kids to have self-esteem. Chuck says, "Kids today can't just say no. How can you tell a young, insecure kid who has no self-confidence to say no to a drug dealer or to someone he looks up to when all his friends are involved? What you have to do is instill that inner strength in him so

At an anti-drug exhibition

Chuck Norris spends time with kids.

he has the courage and confidence to say, 'I don't need that.'"

When he talks to poor kids from broken homes, Chuck can identify with them because he was like them. He tells them his own story, of how martial arts made him feel good about himself. Always, he repeats the theme that martial arts helped him beat the odds.

Besides Kick Drugs out of America, Chuck is involved with several other charities, including Funds for Kids, the Veterans Administration National Salute to Hospitalized Veterans, the Make-a-Wish Foundation, and the United Way.

Currently engaged to

Chuck Norris works out every day.

Monica Hall and a true fitness advocate, Chuck Norris is also a real reserve police officer in Terrell, Texas. In 1996 and 1997, he helped in the arrests of 105 drug suspects. He helped to dismantle three crack-cocaine distribution networks operating in Terrell.

With Monica Hall

Chuck Norris is a man who has fought his way—with grit and determination—to the top. Now the main thing he wants to do is help others, both in the messages of his movies and TV shows and in his efforts to help kids stand up for themselves.

Chuck Norris is a real-life police reserve officer in Terrell, Texas.

Chronology

- Born Carlos Ray Norris on March 10, 1940, in Ryan, Oklahoma, to Wilma Scarberry Norris and Ray Norris
- 1968, graduated from high school in Torrance, California
- December 1958, married Dianne Holechek
- Had two sons, Mike, born in 1963, and Eric, born in 1965
- In 1965 won first national championship in karate
- 1969, first movie role
- 1970, brother Wieland died in Vietnam
- 1979, made first movie that he helped develop—*Good Guys Wear Black.*
- 1990, formed Kick Drugs Out of America
- 1993, became a network TV star with *Walker, Texas Ranger*
- 1998, engaged to Monica Hall

Index

GAYLORD S